TELL ME ABOUT WRITERS

BEATRIX POTTER

written by
John Malam

Evans

Evans Brothers Limited

Published by Evans Brothers Limited
2A Portman Mansions
Chiltern Street
London W1M 1LE

First published 1997

Printed by Graficas Reunidas SA, Spain

British Library Cataloguing in Publication data.

Malam, John
  Tell me about Beatrix Potter
  1. Potter, Beatrix, 1866-1943 – Biography – Juvenile literature
  2. Novelists, English – 20th century – Biography – Juvenile literature
  I. Title II.Beatrix Potter
  823 .9'12

ISBN 0237517612

Beatrix Potter was born in London more than 100 years ago. She liked animals and she had lots of pets. She drew pictures of her animals and made up stories about them. Beatrix became an artist and storyteller. She wrote books for children. She became famous when she wrote a book about a rabbit called Peter.

Beatrix loved to be in the countryside. When she was older she decided to live on a farm in the Lake District. She lived there quietly for the rest of her long life. This is her story.

Beatrix, aged 30

Beatrix Potter's parents were Rupert and Helen. They came from Lancashire, a county in the north of England. Both their families were rich.

Rupert and Helen went to live in London. They had a large house. They had servants to do their cooking and housekeeping.

Beatrix's father, Rupert, was a barrister. But he was rich, so he did not have to work.

Beatrix with her mother, Helen. This photograph was taken by Beatrix's father.

Mr and Mrs Potter called their first child Helen Beatrix. She was born in London on the 28th of July, 1866. She was named Helen after her mother, but people called her by her second name, Beatrix, instead.

When Beatrix was nearly six years old, her brother was born. He was called Bertram.

Beatrix aged 12, with her brother Bertram aged six

Soon after Beatrix was born, a nurse came to live in Mr and Mrs Potter's house. She looked after Beatrix. When Bertram was born she cared for him, too. In those days, children who had rich parents were often brought up by their nurse, not by their parents.

Beatrix spent most of her childhood at home in

the nursery. It was a room high up on the third floor of the house. She had a few toys and some books.

As she grew older, her nurse took her for walks in a park. Sometimes the family's pet dog went with them.

Beatrix painted this picture of the houses in her road.

Even though Beatrix was brought up strictly, she had a happy childhood. She did not have any friends of her own age. Her best friend was her brother. Beatrix became a shy young girl.

Beatrix wrote a diary. To stop other people from reading it, she wrote it in a secret code that only she could read.

Beatrix with Spot, the family spaniel

Caterpillars, drawn by Beatrix when she was nine.

A rabbit, drawn when Beatrix was 13.

Beatrix did not go to school. Instead, the nursery was turned into a classroom and she was taught at home by a governess.

Beatrix and Bertram kept animals in the classroom. They had rabbits, beetles, caterpillars, mice, a frog called Punch, hedgehogs, two lizards called Toby and Judy, bats, newts and a tortoise!

From the age of seven or eight Beatrix began to paint and draw. She liked to make pictures of animals and plants. She was taught about drawing by an art teacher who came to her house.

For many years Beatrix and her family went on holiday to Scotland. The family's servants went too – and so did Beatrix's pets, carefully packed inside little boxes for the long train journey.

Then, when Beatrix was older, she stayed in the Lake District.

Beatrix loved to stay in the Lake District, in the north of England

A new governess came to teach Beatrix when she was sixteen. Her name was Annie Carter. She taught Beatrix how to read, write and speak in German. Annie was only three years older than Beatrix. They became good friends.

When Beatrix was almost nineteen, Annie left to marry an engineer. He was called Edwin Moore. They had eight children.

Beatrix liked painting flowers

Annie Carter, Beatrix's governess and friend

Beatrix often collected mushrooms
and painted them.

After Annie left, Beatrix
felt she was on her own for
the first time in her life. She
had finished her education and
thought about
becoming a
scientist. She had
always been
interested in nature,
especially in toadstools and
mushrooms. She had found out
new facts about how they grew.
She talked to some experts, but
they did not listen to her. At that
time it was very hard for a
woman to become a scientist.

A photograph of Beatrix when she
was 23, taken by her father

Beatrix began to paint pictures of her pets, especially of Benjamin, her rabbit. Her Uncle Henry said her pictures were good enough to sell. A company that made greetings cards bought some of her pictures of rabbits for six pounds. This was a lot of money. The company made her pictures into Christmas cards.

Beatrix with her pet rabbit Benjamin.

Beatrix had kept in touch with her friend Annie. Annie's eldest child was a boy called Noel. When he was five years old, Beatrix wrote a letter to him.

A Christmas card drawn by Beatrix

Noel was poorly and Beatrix wanted to cheer him up. The letter was written in words and pictures. It was about one of her pet rabbits called Peter. The letter began:

My dear Noel,
I don't know what to write to you, so I shall tell you a story about four little rabbits, whose names were Flopsy, Mopsy, Cottontail and Peter.

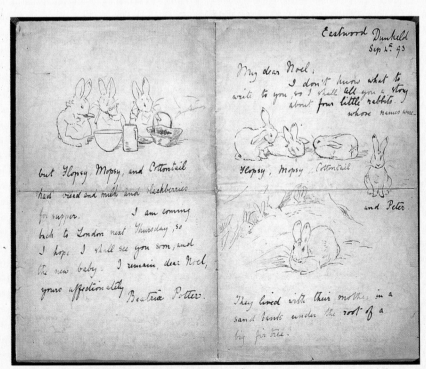

The Peter Rabbit picture letter that Beatrix sent to Noel Moore

Seven years after Beatrix had sent the Peter Rabbit letter to Noel, she wondered if she could make it into a book. Luckily, Noel had kept the letter. Beatrix copied it out neatly and drew new pictures to go with the story.

Beatrix called the story "The Tale of Peter Rabbit". She sent it to six different publishers. None of them wanted to make it into a book. Beatrix decided to do it herself. She paid to have 250 little books made.

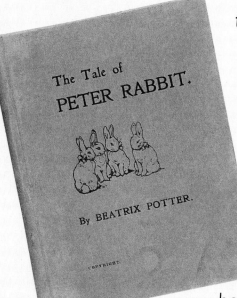

In the book that Beatrix paid to have made, all her pictures were in black and white.

Then, when a publishing
company saw one of her little
books, they said they would
publish it, but only if Beatrix
could do the pictures in colour.
Beatrix was happy to turn her
drawings into colourful pictures.
Beatrix's little book about
Peter Rabbit was a great
success.

In the book that was published
by Frederick Warne & Company,
all the pictures were in colour.

Beatrix wrote more books. Next came "The Tale of Squirrel Nutkin", and then "The Tailor of Gloucester", followed by "The Tale of Benjamin Bunny" and "The Tale of Two Bad Mice". In all, Beatrix wrote and drew the pictures for twenty-three little books.

She became very successful. Beatrix had always enjoyed going on holiday to the Lake District, and so she bought a farm there, in the village of Sawrey. The farm was called Hill Top Farm.

Hill Top Farm in winter, painted by Beatrix

From this moment on, Beatrix began to make great changes to her life. She learned about farming, especially about how to look after sheep.

Beatrix loved the Lake District. She bought other farms and land close to Hill Top Farm. She wanted to keep the land just the way it was, unspoilt by people. She stopped people hunting animals on her land.

William Heelis, a local solicitor, had helped Beatrix to buy her land. Beatrix fell in love with William and they got married. From then on she was called Mrs Heelis.

Beatrix and William Heelis, on their wedding day in 1913

Beatrix Potter died in 1943, after a long and happy life. She was seventy-seven years old.

After Beatrix died, her land and farms in the Lake District were given to the National Trust. Today, the National Trust keeps the land just the way Beatrix had liked it.

Many people visit Hill Top Farm in Sawrey.

Important dates

1866 Helen Beatrix Potter was born in London

1872 Age 6 – Walter Bertram Potter, her brother, was born

1878 Age 12 – an art teacher began to teach her how to draw

1883 Age 16 – her new governess, Annie Carter, arrived

1890 Age 24 – she sold some drawings of rabbits to a company who made them into Christmas cards

1893 Age 27 – she wrote a picture letter to Noel Moore, telling him about a rabbit called Peter

1901 Age 35 – she published "The Tale of Peter Rabbit" herself, with black and white pictures

1902 Age 36 – Frederick Warne & Company published "The Tale of Peter Rabbit", with pictures in colour

1905 Age 39 – she bought Hill Top Farm, at Sawrey in the Lake District

1913 Age 47 – she married William Heelis, a solicitor

1914 Age 47 – her father died, aged 82

1918 Age 52 – her brother died, aged 46

1932 Age 66 – her mother died, aged 93

1943 Age 77 – she died, and her farms and land in the Lake District were given to the National Trust to look after

Keywords

barrister
someone who knows about law and who works in a court

governess
a teacher who teaches children in their own home

publisher
a person or company that makes and sells books

scientist
someone who knows about natural things

Index